FULFILLING WORK

R. PAUL STEVENS & GERRY SCHOBERG

Harold Shaw Publishers
Wheaton, Illinois

Copyright © 1991 by R. Paul Stevens and Gerry Schoberg

All rights reserved. No part of this book may be reproduced or transmitted in any form or by any means, electronic or mechanical, including photocopying, recording, or any information storage and retrieval system without written permission from Harold Shaw Publishers, Box 567, Wheaton, Illinois, 60189. Printed in the United States of America.

ISBN 0-87788-271-1

Cover graphics by Orion Press/FPG International

Cover design by John Seid

99 98 97 96 95 94 93 92 91

10 9 8 7 6 5 4 3 2 1

Contents

How to Use this Discussion Guide _____5

Introduction _____7

Study One/God's Design for Work _____9
Genesis 1:24—2:20

Study Two/Work: Curse or Blessing? _____12
Genesis 2:15-17; 3:1-24

Study Three/Workplace Temptation _____16
Genesis 39:1-23

Study Four/Something Beautiful for God _____20
Exodus 31:1-11

Study Five/Enticed by Riches _____24
Proverbs 22:22-23; 23:10-11; Ecclesiastes 5:8-20

Study Six/Entrepreneurial Homemaking _____28
Proverbs 31:10-31

Study Seven/The Search for Satisfying Work _____32
Ecclesiastes 2:17-26

Study Eight/Heavenly Work _____37
Revelation 4—5

Leader's Notes _____41

Sources and Suggested Reading _____48

How to Use this Discussion Guide

NetWork Discussion Guides are designed for "people on the move." A typical group might use these studies during a lunch break, as part of a fellowship evening in a home, or in a Sunday school class. Each group member should have a copy of this studyguide.

Each study is designed to take about 30 minutes to complete. If you have more than 30 minutes, your group can spend valuable time praying and fellowshiping together.

NetWork studies address important contemporary issues from a biblical perspective. Their ultimate goal is to help you put God's Word into practice in your life. To do this, each study includes three segments.

OPENING IT UP

The study begins with a discussion launcher. This might be a short case study, a provocative quote, or a problem-posing story intended to spark discussion and draw out personal opinion. Spend about 5 minutes on this opener. It will help you to focus on the theme of the study and will help participants to become involved in the discussion.

THINKING IT THROUGH

This section focuses on a Scripture passage, with 4-6 questions that draw out the facts and the meaning of the passage. These thoughtful questions should take about 15 minutes. Background notes on each passage are part of the Leader's Notes.

MAKING IT HAPPEN

This section brings immediacy and concreteness to the issue, with suggestions for life application. Here, group members are encouraged to ask, "So what? What am I going to do about obeying this Scripture in my home or at my job?" Spend about 10 minutes on this important wrap-up.

Each study also features a Journal Entry for follow-up at home. This is another way to make truth personal and active.

You will find additional suggestions for leading the group and helpful notes on each Scripture passage in the Leader's Notes at the back of the guide.

Introduction

> A man can do nothing better than to . . . find satisfaction in his work.—Ecclesiastes 2:24

Daniel Yankelovitch says that we seek a whole new set of satisfactions from our jobs these days: they must be meaningful, appropriate to our talents, facilitating to personal self-development, continuously challenging, and adequately remunerated. ("New Rules," *Psychology Today*, April 1981). It's not surprising that even Christians have trouble saying, "My work is fulfilling."

Within a single generation we have passed from being a survival culture to an identity culture. Today the big question in the workplace is not, "How can I make enough to live and to feed my family?" but, "How can I find out who I am?" Whether overemployed, unemployed, or underemployed, people become identified with their careers or jobs. The first question we often ask each other is, "What do you do?" William Diehl exposes the problem of evaluating ourselves and others on the basis of vocation and performance:

> Without any doubt, the biggest gap between our confessed theology of Sunday and our operational theology of the week is that of works righteousness. On Sunday, we say we believe that God's grace alone has made us a whole and accepted person. On Monday, our actions betray a belief that our identity and work are based entirely on what we do and how well we do it.—*Thank God, It's Monday*

We need to search all of Scripture for answers to our questions about work. God's original design for work is described in Genesis and takes us beyond culture. We'll also learn new perspectives on work from the wisdom literature of the Bible and look at living examples of people in Scripture who faced workplace issues. We pray that these studies will help us focus on Christian responses to the role of work in our lives.

☐ STUDY ONE

GOD'S DESIGN FOR WORK

Genesis 1:24—2:20

OPENING IT UP

In the struggle to find meaning in life, some people put too much into their work, and others put too little. In the late 1970s, the University of Michigan reported that 27 percent of American workers feel so ashamed of the quality of their products that they would not buy them themselves ("New Rules," *Psychology Today*, April 1981). This is work as mere "work"—the exchange of a person's time and talent for money.

At the other extreme, many in our culture are caught up in a neurotic work ethic, letting work define their identity. They are religious about their work. *Time* magazine quoted a former executive of ITT: "It is a whole way of life to work for ITT, like joining a monastic order. That is part of ITT's special strength . . . a feeling you are working for an order and not for a mortal company" (May 1, 1972, p. 52).

Have there been times when you have identified with either of these approaches to work? If so, tell the group about it.

THINKING IT THROUGH

1. Read Genesis 1:24-27. After making everything else and concluding, "It is good," God made human beings. In what ways did God make human beings different from the animals?

He gave human beings a will, mind and emotions and gave us dominion over the creatures of the earth.

2. Read Genesis 1:28—2:3. What unique task did God give to the man and the woman (verse 28)? What activities would be included in this first command?

To be fruitful and multiply. Replish the earth, have dominion over the creatures of the earth. Take care of it.

3. Read Genesis 2:4-20. God adds to the earlier command his injunction to *work* and *take care of* the garden (verse 15). How do these two different words describe humankind's responsibility?

It is our responsibility to take care of those things that God has provided for us.

4. To the ancient Semites, "naming" implied the ability and right to discern the real nature of something and to express authority over it. When God instructed Adam and Eve to name the creatures (verse 19), what did he expect them to do?

Take ownership of them.

GOD'S DESIGN FOR WORK

MAKING IT HAPPEN

Recall a project or task you completed after which you felt like saying, "It was good."

> The Israelites were probably the only people of their day who believed in a God who works. The pattern for their work week—"six days you shall labor . . . but the seventh day is a Sabbath . . ." (Exod. 20:9)—was based on the way God worked in creation.

How would belief in a God who works make one's outlook different from that of the rest of the world?

We want to be like God, so if God works & we remember that he worked when he was here, our attitude will be much different. We work for God, that should make a difference also.

Why is our relationship to God crucial to our attempt to rule and care for the world as godly men and women?

We need to relate our relationship to God first. He is Lord of our life and he takes care of us. Ultimately when we work or supervise we do it like God does it.

In the light of being created by a working God, called to be stewards of the earth, and commanded to build family, why is unemployment a greater problem than just being without a job?

Because unemployment is not is God's will. It breaks down a family rather than build it up.

Journal Entry

Reflect on your present work. How close does it come to reflecting God's purposes for work as described in Genesis 1:24—2:20?

We are to take our assignments and work them diligently recognizing that God gave us the job and we should take it as our own.

☐ STUDY TWO

WORK: CURSE OR BLESSING?

Genesis 2:15-17; 3:1-24

OPENING IT UP

The problem with work is that it usually turns out to be *work*. Our jobs and ministries rarely satisfy completely. Ralph Mattson and Arthur Miller say that "being in a job or role suitable for our gifts is essential in fulfilling God's will. Until the Christian is doing what he should be doing, maturation is hampered" (*Finding a Job You Can Love*). But these authors also report that according to reputable research, three or four out of every five people are in the wrong jobs. Our last study showed that the right job includes being a creative creature. Further study in Genesis shows us why finding the perfect fit is more than just finding the right job.

Recall a work situation which you found particularly frustrating. What made you feel like saying afterwards, "It is *not* good"?

THINKING IT THROUGH

1. Read Genesis 2:15-17. In the previous study we looked at the commission given to humankind to take care of the world. What is the specific command given to Adam? What is the specific limitation?

WORK: CURSE OR BLESSING?

2. God gave Adam freedom in the garden, but he also made him responsible by holding him accountable for his actions. Why are both freedom and responsibility important aspects of any work experience?

3. Read Genesis 3:1-7. In the middle of the garden, God had planted "the tree of the knowledge of good and evil" (2:9), and had told Adam not to eat from it (2:17). After God created Eve as a companion and helper for Adam, the serpent came to tempt her to eat from this tree. What was the serpent really offering Eve?

4. Read Genesis 3:8-19. After God confronted Adam and Eve for their sin, he made three pronouncements: the curse against the serpent (verses 14-15), the effect of sin on the sexual relationship (verse 16), and the curse against the ground (verses 17-19). How exactly would the curse of the ground affect Adam's life?

5. Read Genesis 3:20-24. Do you think that putting the man and woman out of the garden was an act of judgment on God's part, or an act of mercy, or both?

6. What good news for workers is there in this dismissal from the garden?

MAKING IT HAPPEN

Old Testament scholar William Dumbrell states, "By eating the fruit man was intruding into an area reserved for God alone, and the violation of the command is tantamount to an assertion of equality with God, a snatching at deity" *(Covenant and Creation)*. How does this same temptation express itself to you in the workplace?

> In *Finding a Job You Can Love*, Ralph Mattson and Arthur Miller address the matter of compulsively pursuing our own vision and insisting on our own way. "We not only want to do what we want how and when we want, but we also want our desires to have priority over everyone else's . . . We are competing with God, a contest we are sure to lose, but one we take on nevertheless."

In what ways if any does Genesis 3:14-19 affect the distinctive vocation of humankind that we discovered in the previous study; i.e., that human beings were created in the image of God and that they were given the task to take care of the world (1:27-28; 2:7, 15)?

WORK: CURSE OR BLESSING?

From what you have learned so far, what do you think would have to happen before the curse on creation could be removed so that human beings could fulfill their mandate without "painful toil"?

How has studying this passage of Scripture helped you to deal with the frustrations you experience in your own work?

Journal Entry

What roles do freedom and responsibility play in your life and work? Commit both your freedoms and responsibilities to God, asking him to show you his purposes for both.

☐ STUDY THREE

WORKPLACE TEMPTATION

Genesis 39:1-23

OPENING IT UP

Work is the daily invasion of the Christian influence into the world. But there is no job or ministry that is free from temptation. There are so many opportunities for sin! A company might keep double books, an industry might meet no genuine human need, an organization might advance people through financial or sexual favors or develop a product that brings great income through third-world exploitation.

Describe a work situation in which you were tempted to compromise in behavior or ethics.

WORKPLACE TEMPTATION

THINKING IT THROUGH

Joseph was the favorite son of the patriarch Jacob. His brothers, jealous of their father's favors toward Joseph, tried to eliminate him by selling him to Midianite traders. Joseph became a slave—the personal servant of Potiphar, an important Egyptian official.

1. Read Genesis 39:1-6a. Why was Joseph successful in Potiphar's house?

2. Read Genesis 39:6b-20a. What factors would make this temptation particularly difficult to resist?

3. How might Joseph's career in Potiphar's house have been advanced or restricted if he had chosen a different way to handle this temptation?

4. What does Joseph say and do in order to deal victoriously with temptation that is attractive, repeated, and demanding?

5. Read Genesis 39:20b-23. How was Joseph's faithfulness under trial rewarded?

Joseph interpreted the dreams of two important fellow-prisoners. Because of this, Joseph was introduced to Pharaoh and became his assistant in guiding Egypt through seven years of famine, thus enabling Joseph to save the lives of his family who came to Egypt looking for food. Eventually Joseph could say to his astonished brothers, "You intended to harm me, but God intended it for good to accomplish what is now being done, the saving of many lives" (Gen. 50:20).

MAKING IT HAPPEN

> Temptations that find us dwelling in God are to our faith like winds that more firmly root the tree.—Anonymous

Identify some of the temptations you encounter in the workplace. How can Joseph's example help you cope with temptations (pride, lust, idolatry, greed, etc.) in the context of work?

How does Joseph's imprisonment for his faithfulness give a real, though disturbing, answer to those who claim that following Jesus will make you wealthy, healthy, and happy?

In what practical way(s) is Joseph a good example of a person doing what God mandated (Gen. 1:26-28)?

Not every Christian experiences success and prosperity as a result of faithfulness under trial. How does Joseph's experience help us trust God in difficult work situations when we cannot imagine a wonderful ending for our own stories?

Journal Entry

What inner disciplines would have kept Joseph from bitterness when he was let down so many times? Which one of these disciplines do you need to ask God for now?

☐ STUDY FOUR

SOMETHING BEAUTIFUL FOR GOD

Exodus 31:1-11

OPENING IT UP

Three stone masons working in a quarry were asked what they were doing. One said, "I am cutting stones." The second replied, "I am earning money." But the third answered, "I am building a cathedral."

It is easier for us to define our work by its task or its financial reward than by how it keeps with the vision of building the kingdom of God. For many of us, work is neither inspired nor inspiring. Instead of building cathedrals we have to work for God as we build an office complex, fill out order forms, or do the laundry.

As you look back over your life, what is the most inspiring task, work, or project you have undertaken? What made that task so inspiring?

SOMETHING BEAUTIFUL FOR GOD

THINKING IT THROUGH

Exodus 19—40 contains the instructions given to Moses about how the Old Covenant people were to live, worship, and work. Exodus 31:1-11 describes the God-directed construction of the tabernacle and its furnishings. This sacred tent was a portable meeting place with God (Exod. 25:8, 22), suitable for the Lord's people moving through the wilderness after being saved out of Egypt.

1. **Read Exodus 31:1-11.** What exactly did God direct Bezalel, Oholiab, and the other craftsmen to make?

2. The building of a tabernacle appears to be a holy task, similar to professional Christian ministry today. However, what parts of the task would be made difficult because of the Fall?

3. How was Oholiab's job of helping Bezalel like so many jobs people have today?

4. From verse 1-11, compare the actions taken by God and the actions taken by the people. What relationship exists here between obedience and the Spirit's enabling?

MAKING IT HAPPEN

> The Church's approach to an intelligent carpenter is usually confined to exhorting him not to be drunk and disorderly in his leisure hours, and to come to church on Sundays. What the Church should be telling him is this: that the very first demand that his religion makes upon him is that he should make good tables. Church by all means, and decent forms of amusement, certainly—but what use is all that if in the very center of his life and occupation he is insulting God with bad carpentry? . . . The only Christian work is a good work well done.—Dorothy Sayers, *Why Work?*

Bezalel is the only Old Testament person described as "filled . . . with the Spirit of God" (Exod. 31:3). What difference will it make in your work to know that your talents and abilities are given to you by the Holy Spirit?

How can Bezalel's example inspire Christians to work for God where they are, whether in remunerated work or personal creativity?

> God didn't stop working after Creation. He continues to work, upholding the creation (Col. 1:16-17, Heb. 1:3). He also meets His creatures' many needs (Psalm 104). He is working out His purposes in History (e.g., Dt. 11:1-7). And of course He accomplished the great work of Atonement at the Cross . . .
>
> God is a worker. This alone tells us that work must be significant, that it must have *intrinsic* value. For by definition, God can do nothing that is not inherently good, or else He would violate His own nature and character. The fact that God calls what He does work and calls it good means that work has intrinsic worth. —Doug Sherman and William Hendricks, *Discipleship Journal*

Journal Entry

Read Psalm 111, noting what it says about God's works. Write down your thoughts of praise to God as the psalmist does. Offer your whole life, including your work, as an act of worship to God.

☐ STUDY FIVE

ENTICED BY RICHES

*Proverbs 22:22-23; 23:10-11;
Ecclesiastes 5:8-20*

OPENING IT UP

Students of the 60s and 70s protested the evils they saw in the world with slogans like "Make love not war." But today, in place of the idealism of the past, there is a quest for experience and luxury, typified in the slogan "You can have it all." The Yuppie has replaced the Hippie, bringing a new challenge to the church.

> Baptizing the Yuppie mentality with a Christian vocabulary is one form of our cultural conformity. The logic is strikingly simple: God calls us to excellence; we must commit ourselves to exceptional performance in our jobs, even if it means sacrifice, and we will be blessed by all the benefits of career advancement. What we have done, of course, is empty these words (excellence, sacrifice, and blessing) of their biblical content and pour in the world's meaning.—John A. Bernbaum and Simon M. Steer, *Why Work?*

How do you react when someone challenges your lifestyle?

THINKING IT THROUGH

Let's look at the wisdom of the Israelite sages as we consider a kingdom lifestyle.

1. Read Proverbs 22:22-23. Why are the poor attractive prey for exploitation?

2. Concern for the poor is an issue in any society. We do not have to look to the "third world" to see the evidence of poverty; every society has poor people. If the positive counterpart of verse 22 is to help the poor, how can we do this practically?

3. How might helping the poor affect one's personal ambitions?

As a safeguard against developing a class society of rich vs. poor, a provision was written right into the law whereby a poor person could sell his property, but it had to be returned to him in the Year of Jubilee (Lev. 25:23-28). Thus, moving a boundary stone shows a lack of concern for this insurance against poverty and a lack of concern for the poor. Moving a boundary stone made the change of property ownership permanent, and permanent change left the poor with no hope of recovery. No one would try to move the boundary stone of someone who could retaliate; only those who were defenseless were open to this kind of violation (Prov. 23:10).

4. Read Proverbs 23:10-11. How might the instruction not to move a boundary stone be expressed in today's world?

MAKING IT HAPPEN

Read Ecclesiastes 5:8-20. What is it that riches appear to offer that only God can offer (verses 10-11)?

Most Christians struggle with the tension between trusting God to supply their needs and using their own resources to do the same. On the one hand, Jesus taught us not to worry but to trust God to supply all our material needs (Matt. 6:25-34). On the other hand, sitting around seldom gets things done. How can we resolve this tension of working for a living and yet living in honest dependence on God?

What can you learn from this passage about the relationship between contentment and money?

> Contentment is the secret of inward peace. It remembers the stark truth that we brought nothing into the world and we can take nothing out of it. Life, in fact, is a pilgrimage from one moment of nakedness to another. So we should travel light and live simply. Our enemy is not possessions, but excess. Our battle cry is not "Nothing!" but "Enough!" We've got enough. Simplicity says, if we have food and clothing, we will be content with that.—John Stott, *Discipleship Journal*

Journal Entry

> Your checkbook reveals all that you really believe about stewardship. A life story could be written from a checkbook.
> —Ron Blue, *Discipleship Journal*

If a stranger were looking at your check register, what conclusions might that person draw about your lifestyle and what is important to you? Spend some time looking at the entries in your checkbook and ask yourself if your priorities are being guided by Scripture. As you commit your finances to God, is there anything on which you should be spending less money? More? Reflect on 1 Timothy 6:6-8 and list some steps you could take toward learning contentment with whatever God gives you.

☐ STUDY SIX

ENTREPRENEURIAL HOMEMAKING

Proverbs 31:10-31

OPENING IT UP

Societal roles for women have changed radically in this century, partly because women have experienced greater frustration than men in their search for fulfilling work. In the typical Christian stereotype, the male pursues a career in society and the female keeps the home. Our study of Proverbs 31 will show that many modern Christians have not yet caught up with the Old Testament, let alone the New!

Describe how you think women's roles in society have changed in the last thirty years.

THINKING IT THROUGH

1. Read Proverbs 31:10-31. Put in your own words the various ways the noble wife cares for her household.

# ENTREPRENEURIAL HOMEMAKING 29

2. What do you think this passage says about the values, dignity, and opportunities of being a homemaker?

3. What sorts of things does this noble wife do outside the home?

4. The worth of a particular kind of work is often measured by the pay associated with it. Of all the things that this noble wife does, which ones does she get paid for and which ones are volunteer labor?

5. The husband of this noble wife is very much in the background in this passage. What can you tell about their relationship?

MAKING IT HAPPEN

> People who pronounce that it is only woman whose place is in the home forget that in the beginning home and workplace were one for both man and woman. Many occupational distinctions we now make simply did not apply in the most ancient times. Our twentieth century money-dependent society is vastly different from the dawn of human history!
>
> The earliest people produced their own food, manufactured their own clothing, and built their own shelter. . . . All able-bodied family members were needed, and all but the very rich or powerful engaged in work activities.—Gretchen Gaebelein Hull, *Equal to Serve: Women and Men in the Church and Home*

In ancient Israel, as in many oriental cultures today, the family unit was highly valued. Some say that the value of housework has been degraded in our society because the family is no longer highly valued. Do you agree or disagree? Why?

What would you say are the major life goals of the noble wife in Proverbs 31? How do you think she measures the worthiness of her work?

This passage begins as though it were a husband reflecting on the value of his wife. He says that a noble wife "is worth far more than rubies." What does this say about the husband's values?

How does the picture of the wife in Proverbs 31 challenge the ideal picture of a woman in today's society?

Journal Entry

> Where should women serve the Lord? The answers are as many as the places on earth. While a woman's ministry need not be limited to her home, it must always begin there. Then it will reach out in ever-widening circles, according to the Acts 1:8 principle: But you will receive power when the Holy Spirit comes on you; and you will be my witnesses in Jerusalem, and in all Judea, and Samaria, and to the ends of the earth.—Kari Torjesen Malcolm, *Women at the Crossroads*

List a variety of jobs that are associated with the smooth running of a household. Make a note of the skills and character qualities necessary if a person is to contribute substantially to a family. How are these different from and similar to attributes and skills required in the average workplace?

☐ STUDY SEVEN

THE SEARCH FOR SATISFYING WORK

Ecclesiastes 2:17-26

OPENING IT UP

A Ford welfare worker recounted a revealing conversation he once had with an assembly line worker in Detroit:

"What are you making?" he asked.
"C 429," came the bored reply.
"What is C 429?"
"I don't know."
"How long have you been making C 429?"
"Nine years."

If such meaninglessness were confined to assembly-line jobs, the solution would be technology—replacing human beings with robots for routine, repetitive jobs. But meaninglessness infects all work at some point, even professional, people-helping occupations and the Christian ministry. Homemakers especially struggle with work that never seems to be finished. This is the dark side of work—sometimes it seems useless. The problem is multiplied for people who find their identity in what they do rather than who they are, because meaningless work produces meaningless persons.

Describe in as much detail as you can remember some work experience of emptiness or futility you have had.

THINKING IT THROUGH

1. Read Ecclesiastes 2:17-26. Why does the Teacher say he hates life?

2. The theme of vanity runs throughout the book. What reason does the Teacher give for his frustration in the search for satisfying work?

3. How is it possible to work with "wisdom, knowledge and skill" and yet find the work meaningless and be left in despair?

4. The Teacher is describing his search for satisfying work "under the sun" (verses 17-18). By describing meaningless toil exclusively in the observable world (without reference to a supreme being), what is the Teacher inviting us to consider?

5. In verse 24 there is a change of mood. What has the compulsive worker been missing with his days of toil and nights of worry?

6. In verse 26 the Teacher introduces the positive note on which he later ends the whole book. How is this assurance different from the modern "gospel of affluence" which promises that believers will be spared hardships, risks, and poverty?

7. In both verses 21 and 26 the worker has wisdom and knowledge. How does the Teacher account for their very different experience of work?

MAKING IT HAPPEN

> If it were desired to reduce a man to nothing, it would be necessary only to give his work a character of uselessness.—Dostoevski

By pushing his audience's thoughts beyond the comfort zone, the Teacher apparently intends to awaken hunger for God. In your life, how has plumbing the depths of an empty experience led to strengthened faith?

The writer of Ecclesiastes looks back over his life and tries to find some meaning in all the work he has done. Workaholics have a similar response in that life to them is work and work is life. What is the difference between working "wholeheartedly, as if you were serving the Lord" (Eph. 6:7) and being a workaholic?

Many people leave so-called "secular" work and go into Christian ministry in search of satisfying and meaningful work. What would make even Christian ministry ultimately meaningless?

What advice would you give to an assembly-line worker (like the maker of C 429) to help him find satisfaction in his work?

> Since everything about you should be involved in loving God, it makes sense that your work should be involved as well. Just think about how much of your heart, soul, mind, and strength go into your work. Imagine, then, as you spend yourself at that task, being able to say, "I'm here to do something God wants done, and I intend to do it because I love Him.
> ... Looking at work this way can revolutionize our attitudes and behavior on the job. Perhaps for the first time, we'll see a connection between what we do all day and what God wants done. In other words, we'll become coworkers with God in the everyday tasks of life.—Doug Sherman and William Hendricks, *Discipleship Journal*

Journal Entry

Is the job you are doing something God wants done in the world? If so, ask God to help you love him through your work. Write Colossians 3:23-24 in your journal. What changes in behavior or attitude do you need to make in order to carry out your job "as working for the Lord, not for men"?

☐ Study Eight

HEAVENLY WORK
Revelation 4—5

OPENING IT UP

Malcolm Muggeridge once said that only the heavenly minded are of any earthly use. The hope of heaven takes us beyond culture and history to our ultimate destiny in the presence of God. John's vision of heaven in Revelation 4 and 5 is perhaps our most important study on work. By discovering our ultimate destiny we can make appropriate goals here on earth—goals in harmony with the purposes of Christ's kingdom. With kingdom-consciousness, we *will* be of earthly use.

What do you picture yourself doing in heaven?

THINKING IT THROUGH

1. Read Revelation 4. This is an attempt at the impossible: the "description" of God. The passage is intended not simply to describe God, but to evoke faith and response. What are some of the impressions you have in reading this?

2. The four living creatures (verses 6-8) represent wild animals, domesticated animals, flying creatures, and people. What work occupies these creatures (verse 8) and the twenty-four elders (verse 11)?

3. If this is a partial picture of heavenly activity, what dimensions of human senses, communication, and movement will be engaged?

In chapter 5, John grants us a further look through the open door (4:1) into heaven, but this time the cause of worship is God's determination to bring human history to a worthy end, as symbolized by the opening of the scroll and its seals.

4. Read Revelation 5. The Lion has triumphed (verse 5), but then the image of the Lion dissolves into a slain Lamb (verse 6). What does this tell us about the nature of the ultimate victory of the kingdom of God?

5. Those redeemed in Christ become "a kingdom and priests to serve our God, and they will reign on the earth" (verse 10). In what ways is this vision a fulfillment of God's original mandate for humankind in Genesis 1 and 2?

6. From chapters 4 and 5, how do we already know that our ultimate destiny is not eternal passivity but dynamism and creativity?

It is useless to speculate how the saints will ultimately reign on earth, but it is profitable to anticipate the possibility that every worthwhile human activity on earth will find its appropriate and ultimate expression—whether artistic, cultural, intellectual, scientific, manual, or social—in God's reign!

MAKING IT HAPPEN

> Heaven is not static or boring because it is not the end but the beginning, not the evening but the morning, not a warm, womblike bath but a cold, birthlike shower.—Peter Kreeft, *Heaven, the Heart's Deepest Desire*

What difference can the heavenly vision of worship in Revelation make in our struggle to find fulfilling work right now?

What concrete steps have you made toward seeing daily work as a way to worship God?

Journal Entry

A biblical view of work can be summed up in this ancient aphorism: *prayer is work and work is prayer.* Another way to express this is that the ministry of work must never be separated from the work of ministry.

As you reflect on your own work, how have these studies helped you to develop new perspectives about what makes that work fulfilling?

Leader's Notes

As leader of your group, one of your key roles is to keep the discussion on target. You don't need to be an expert or an answer person—your responsibility is to ask, not tell. The questions in the discussion guide will help you to facilitate meaningful discussion.

NetWork Discussion Guides provide spaces between questions for jotting down responses, comments, and related questions you would like to raise in the group. Each group member should have a copy of the guide and may take a turn in leading your group.

This studyguide is based on the **New International Version** of the Bible. Encourage group members to use any accurate, modern translation as the basis for study and discussion.

Preparing to Lead

1. Read and study the Bible passage and related material thoroughly beforehand, asking God to help you understand and apply the passage to your own life.

2. Pray for each member of your group, asking God to prepare each one for the life-changing truth of the study.

3. Familiarize yourself with the leader's notes for the study you are leading. These notes provide you with background information and comments about some of the questions. Use the space below the questions to make notes of helpful ideas.

Leading the Study

1. Begin (and end) the study promptly.

2. Lead in prayer or ask someone ahead of time to open with prayer.

3. Explain that your study format will be a discussion, not a lecture. Encourage everyone to participate, but don't push those who are hesitant to speak in the first few sessions.

4. Read the discussion launcher (OPENING IT UP) out loud and discuss the accompanying question.

5. Read the Bible passage aloud, or ask a volunteer to read it. Then ask each question in the THINKING IT THROUGH section, encouraging all to participate. Don't be afraid of silence. Allow time for thoughtful answers.

6. Don't answer your own questions. If necessary, repeat or rephrase questions until they are clearly understood.

7. If a question comes up that you can't answer, don't be afraid to admit you're baffled! Assign the topic as a research project for someone to report on the next time you meet.

8. When tangents are introduced, bring the discussion back to the topic at hand. Sometimes, of course, tangents are important. Be sensitive to the Holy Spirit and to the needs of your group.

9. Be sure to leave adequate time for the application questions in MAKING IT HAPPEN. The goal of these studies is changed lives!

10. End your discussion with specific, personal prayer for each other, asking God to help you obey the Scripture you studied.

Study One/God's Design for Work

Purpose: to discover God's intended relationship between human beings and work in his world.

LEADER'S NOTES

Question 2. Only human beings are commanded to "subdue" and "rule" (verse 28). Draw suggestions from the group about how the "creation mandate" may be fulfilled in contexts other than a garden.

Question 3. The word "work" in Hebrew carries the idea of service, and even slavery. The word "care" in Hebrew means to be very careful to guard something. God's commission to rule and subdue (1:28) is combined with the command to work and to care for (2:15). Human beings are not to be distant or disinterested autocrats, but servant-leaders who are personally interested in creation.

Study Two/Work: Curse or Blessing?

Purpose: to understand the effect of sin in relation to our work.

Question 1. The nature of Adam's work was both freedom and responsibility (2:16-17). Adam was free to enjoy and order creation as he chose (2:19-20). But along with the freedom came accountability and restriction. Be aware of the dangerous half-truth that we are free when we have no limits.

Question 2. Freedom means that people can be creative in their work and can develop a sense of "ownership" by being able to "do it their way." To be accountable means that people will suffer the consequences if they do not perform their specific tasks. Few workplaces have an ideal mixture of freedom and accountability, but the ideal should challenge both supervisors and employees.

Question 3. Focus on the content of the temptation. Both the serpent (3:5) and God (3:22) make statements that suggest there was more to the tree than a test of obedience. The eater would be enlightened, "like God knowing good and evil" (3:5). The *knowledge of good and evil* is something God-given and is necessary for those who rule in a world where both good and evil occur. Adam and Eve did not need the knowledge of good and evil to fulfill their commission because there was no evil in their world.

Study Three/Workplace Temptation

Purpose: to show how temptation in the marketplace can be overcome.

Question 4. Draw out the specifics of how Joseph handled this sexual temptation: he reminded himself and the woman of the exact nature of his responsibility, of her rightful loyalty, of the exact nature of the anticipated deed, and of the One to whom he was ultimately accountable.

MAKING IT HAPPEN. Your group should be concerned with all appeals to the flesh in the marketplace—not just sexual temptation. Encourage group members to apply these same principles to other, more subtle, seductions. Reassure them with the New Testament promise of 1 Corinthians 10:13.

Explore with your group the good things God can bring out of unfavorable circumstances (Rom. 8:28). Encourage each other to see the greater value of maturity and faith over material prosperity.

Study Four/Something Beautiful for God

Purpose: to show how even "non-spiritual" work can be inspired by the Holy Spirit for the glory of God.

Question 2. Even this extraordinary holy project had some elements of drudgery—the preparation of the materials, the frustration of parts that did not fit together as planned, mistakes, and disagreements about what artistic expression best conveyed Israel's spirituality.

Question 3. Oholiab played a "second-fiddle" role.

MAKING IT HAPPEN. Though no other text in the Old Testament describes a person as being "filled with the Spirit," there were undoubtedly many others who were (1 Sam. 16:13). What the Old Testament "elite" experienced is now the privilege of every Christian who experiences in Jesus the continuous filling of the Holy Spirit (Eph. 1:13; Gal. 5:22-25). In this case, the builder of the tabernacle, not the priest within it, was singled out as being Spirit-inspired.

Study Five/Enticed by Riches

Purpose: to examine values that should concern people who want to get ahead in their workplace.

LEADER'S NOTES

Question 1. In Proverbs, attitude toward the poor is very important. The righteous person will help the poor (29:7) because he sees this as service to God (19:17), and he is blessed (22:9). However, those who take advantage of the poor for their own gain will eventually come to poverty themselves (22:16, 22) and disregard for the poor shows disregard for God (14:31).

Question 2. Help group members personalize the question about practically helping the poor. A number of good general suggestions may be offered, but lead people to see how they can be personally involved. Perhaps the group as a whole could also work to this end (e.g. volunteering to work at a mission, organizing a food bank in the church, sponsoring a child, etc.).

Study Six/Entrepreneurial Homemaking

Purpose: to establish the dignity of homemaking, and to show that the woman who embraces this vocation is not bound to the home.

This passage in Proverbs is an acrostic poem, meaning that in Hebrew the first letters of all the verses make up the alphabet. Therefore, the various characteristics of the wife are woven throughout the poem.

Question 3. This question challenges the traditional view of the woman being "confined" to the home. The noble wife is involved in buying a field *on her own initiative* and *with her own earnings* she plants a vineyard (verse 16), suggesting that she not only has a degree of independence in what she does, but also that she has income other than what her husband brings home (verses 18, 24). Verse 26 says that she speaks with wisdom, which further implies that she is well educated.

MAKING IT HAPPEN. In contrast to many women in our society, the noble wife in Proverbs seems to find her purpose for life in what she does for others. Though a number of her activities may be personally satisfying in themselves, it is significant that they focus on the needs of other people.

Study Seven/The Search for Satisfying Work

Purpose: to show that work becomes meaningless when we try to get out of it what we should be finding in our relationship with God.

Question 1. The person who says, "I hate life" may be closer to faith than the person who has never thought deeply enough about life to wonder and question.

Question 3. Some work has meaning only in terms of the kingdom of God.

Question 4. The Teacher is pressing us to think about the meaninglessness of work when a person has no divine reference point. By inviting us to examine work as it is without faith, the Teacher hopes to provoke a longing for the God without whom there is no meaning.

Question 5. The worker has missed time for rest and recreation, acknowledging God's gift of refreshment.

Question 6. Derek Kidner's comments on this verse are superb: "The fact that in the end the sinner's hoard will go to the righteous is only a crowning irony to what was in any case *vanity and striving after wind.* And for the righteous it is a crowning vindication, but no more. Like the meek, who are promised the earth, their treasure is elsewhere and of another kind" *(A Time To Mourn and A Time To Dance).*

MAKING IT HAPPEN. Workaholics (1) cannot rest, (2) fill leisure time with thoughts of and plans for work, (3) are identified with their work and judge their success or failure on the basis of work performance, (4) are motivated in their compulsion by the darker side of their personalities (pride, the desire for power and status), and (5) are using work to fill the soul's God-shaped vacuum which was designed to be filled through intentional, loving relationship with God. Even though Christians can be aggressive and passionate workers and share *some* of these dimensions, they are subject to the call of God and can be redeemed into passionate and holy work.

LEADER'S NOTES

Study Eight/Heavenly Work

Purpose: to discover the relevance of our heavenly homeland to our struggle for fulfillment in work now.

Question 3. Group members will note that we will use all the human senses to absorb the sights and sounds of heavenly worship and that we will use our voices (singing) and our bodies (kneeling, falling down, laying crowns) to worship.

Question 4. Your group can find immense encouragement from the truth that the Lamb will ultimately triumph. History will end with the glorious consummation of the kingdom of God and the coming of our God and Savior, Jesus Christ. But ultimate victory is costly. Your group could reflect on how work on earth, with influences from the world, the flesh, and the devil, cannot be redeemed by human effort. Human fulfillment is blood-bought.

MAKING IT HAPPEN. Help your group to see work as one way to worship the Lord here on earth.

Sources and Suggested Reading

Bernbaum, John A. and Simon M. Steer. *Why Work?* Grand Rapids: Baker Book House, 1986.

Blue, Ron. "Money: If God Owns It All, What Are You Doing With It?" *Discipleship Journal*, Issue 53.

Diehl, William E. *Thank God, It's Monday.* Philadelphia: Fortress Press, 1982.

Dumbrell, William. *Covenant and Creation.* Exeter, Devon: Paternoster Press, 1984.

Gibbs, Mark. *Christians with Secular Power.* Philadelphia: Fortress Press, 1981.

Hull, Gretchen Gaebelein. *Equal to Serve: Women and Men in the Church and Home.* Old Tappan, N.J.: Fleming H. Revell Company, 1987.

Kreeft, Peter. *Heaven, the Heart's Deepest Desire.* San Francisco: Ignatius Press, 1989.

Malcolm, Kari Torjesen. *Women at the Crossroads.* Downers Grove, Ill.: InterVarsity Press, 1982.

Mattson, Ralph and Arthur Miller. *Finding a Job You Can Love.* Nashville: Thomas Nelson, 1982.

Mouw, Richard. *Called to Holy Worldliness.* Philadelphia: Fortress Press, 1980.

Sherman, Doug and William Hendricks. "Does Your Job Matter?" *Discipleship Journal*, Issue 45.

Slocum, Robert. *Ordinary Christians in a High-Tech World.* Waco, Tex.: Word Books, 1986.

Stott, John. As quoted in Steve Thurman's "Life, Liberty, and the Pursuit of Just a Little More" in *Discipleship Journal*, Issue 53.